A New True Book

FLOODS

By Arlene Erlbach

Acknowledgment
David Hunter, P.E. Project Manager, Programs/Project Management,
Division of U.S. Army Corps of Engineers, Chicago District

CHILDRENS PRESS®

CHICAGO

A truck is trapped by floodwaters
on a Chicago expressway.

Dedicated to the Saturday Critique Group

PHOTO CREDITS

The Bettmann Archive–14, 34 (top right)

© Cameramann International, Ltd.–2, 29 (left), 36 (2 photos), 38

H. Armstrong Roberts–© D. Carriere, 4 (bottom)

Photri–12, 31 (left), 33 (right); © James Kirby, 9; © H. Hungerford, 20

Reuters/Bettmann–10, 26 (right), 28

Root Resources–© Garry D. McMichael, Cover, 7, (left), 44-45; © Steve Crook, 26 (left), 43

© Scott T. Smith–23 (left)

SuperStock International, Inc.–4

Tony Stone Images–© Jerald P. Fish, 41

UPI/Bettmann–14 (inset), 24 (2 photos), 34 (left and bottom right)

Valan–© Harold V. Green, 6; © Richard Nowitz, 7 (right); © Tom W. Parkin, 8, 32 (left); © John Eastcott/Yva Momatiuk, 11; © Francis Lepine, 17; © Val & Alan Wilkinson, 19; © Stephen Krasemann, 23 (right); © J. R. Page, 29 (right); © Kennon Cooke, 31 (right); © R. Moller, 40

© Map art by John Forsberg–4

COVER: Flooded Newport, Arkansas

Project Editor: Fran Dyra
Design: Margrit Fiddle

Library of Congress Cataloging-in-Publication Data

Erlbach, Arlene.
    Floods / by Arlene Erlbach.
        p.   cm.–(A New true book)
    Includes index.
    ISBN 0-516-01067-0
    1.   Floods–Juvenile literature.   [1.   Floods.]
I.   Title.
GB1399.E75   1994
551.48'.9–dc20   94-14394
                                                                           CIP
                                                                           AC

TABLE OF CONTENTS

Eastern
Hemisphere

Western
Hemisphere

Water covers 70 percent of the Earth's surface.
During river floods (above), water covers
the surrounding land. Ocean waves (below) can
cause flooding of coastal areas.

WATER EVERYWHERE

Water covers 70 percent of the Earth's surface. It fills all our rivers, lakes, and oceans.

Sometimes rivers overflow their banks. Sometimes ocean waves roll onto land. When water flows over places that are normally dry, it causes a flood. Floods are common and natural occurrences. They happen all over the world.

Flooded farmland in Ontario, Canada

FLOODPLAINS

Areas of land along rivers are called floodplains. Many people like to live on or near floodplains. Many farms have been located close to rivers because floods can bring valuable minerals to the soil. These minerals help crops grow.

Riverboats and barges provide transportation for people and goods. This is why many towns and cities have been built on rivers.

Barge traffic on the Mississippi River at St. Louis (left) and boats on the River Thames, London, England (right)

People use rivers for boating and swimming.

Some people live on rivers because they enjoy swimming, boating, and fishing. And houses built near water often have lovely settings and beautiful views.

Many floodplains flood regularly, and the floods usually cause little

Floodwaters covered the streets of Harpers Ferry, Virginia, in the spring of 1985.

damage. But some floods can be dangerous and destructive. Major floods can wash away buildings, houses, and cars. They can destroy crops. And people and animals may drown in floodwaters.

In the United States,

Cars and buses—and people—are often caught
in sudden floods from torrential rains.

floods kill more people
than any other weather-
related event. Floods
cause billions of dollars of
damage throughout the
world each year. Major
floods are one of the
world's most serious
natural disasters.

COASTAL FLOODS

When people hear about floods, they often think of rivers flooding. But areas near the ocean flood, too. This is called seacoast, or coastal, flooding.

High waves pushed up by hurricanes flood towns along the coasts.

Tsunami waves can flood shorelines very suddenly, causing death and destruction.

Sometimes coastal flooding is caused by a *tsunami*, or tidal wave. Tsunamis begin when an earthquake occurs on the ocean floor or when a seafloor volcano erupts.

The sudden jolt of the earthquake or eruption

disturbs the seafloor. That disturbance causes waves in the ocean. The waves travel outward from the source at speeds of up to 500 miles (805 kilometers) per hour.

In the open ocean, tsunami waves may be only 3 feet (1 meter) high. But when they reach shallow water near shore, the waves rise to 100 feet (30 meters) or more. Tsunamis cause massive flooding, destruction, and death.

Hurricanes cause devastating winds and high waves.
Meteorologists track hurricanes to try to predict their
course. Satellite photos (inset) help them see the
shape and direction of the storm.

A hurricane may cause
coastal flooding, too.
Hurricanes are huge,
whirling rainstorms that
form over oceans and
travel toward land. The
winds in hurricanes reach

speeds as high as 150 miles (241 kilometers) per hour.

A hurricane's winds and rain push ocean waves up to 20 feet (6 meters) high. When these waves smash onto shore, the water flows across land for miles. This is called a storm surge. Most hurricane deaths occur in storm surges.

A hurricane's heavy rains deposit huge amounts of water on the land. This also causes coastal flooding.

RIVER FLOODS

River floods occur when a river or stream overflows. Rivers and streams are long, flowing, bodies of water that are usually lower than the land around them.

When rain falls, the ground soaks up some of the water. Trees and other plants absorb it through their roots. And some water seeps underground and becomes groundwater.

Floodwaters spread far and wide when the Richelieu River in Quebec, Canada, overflows.

But if too much rain falls, the soil becomes saturated. The ground cannot absorb all of it.

The extra water flows downhill into a river or stream and is carried to the ocean. But sometimes too much water flows into

17

a river or stream at one time. The river water rises higher and higher.

Finally, the river overflows its banks. Then the water floods onto the land.

Melting snow can cause floods, too. In the spring, the air warms. Heavy winter snows melt. But if the ground is still frozen, it cannot absorb water. The meltwater then flows into rivers and streams.

In spring, the meltwater from deep winter snows can cause a river to flood.

If too much melted snow flows into a river, the river rises over its banks. The height at which the river water begins to flow across the land is called the flood stage.

When a river is rising, people pile sandbags on
the banks to try to hold back the water.

FLASH FLOODS

It usually takes several
weeks of heavy rains for
rivers to reach flood stage.
People who live near such
rivers can prepare for the
flood and protect themselves.

But sometimes heavy rains cause a flash flood. Flash floods are sudden and extremely dangerous. Most flood deaths occur during flash floods.

Flash floods strike when rain falls in a torrential downpour. For example, cloudbursts from severe thunderstorms have caused many flash floods. The heavy rains of hurricanes can also cause flash floods.

During a severe rainstorm, water falls so fast that the ground cannot absorb it all. In a heavy downpour, an area may get as much rain in a few hours as it normally gets in a year.

Then, millions of gallons of water pour swiftly into rivers and streams. A tiny stream can quickly become a raging river.

Muddy water from a flash flood flows over a cliff that is normally dry (left). Small streams quickly become raging torrents during a flash flood (right).

The river cannot carry the water away fast enough. Soon, with little warning, rivers and streams overflow.

In 1976, a flash flood in Colorado caused 139

The Big Thompson River flood of 1976 washed out roads and
swept away cars and buildings. At right, a rescue worker
looks for victims in the floodwaters.

deaths and major destruction.
The Big Thompson River
overflowed after five hours
of heavy rain. The downpour
caused the usually shallow
river to rise over 20 feet
(6 meters).

HOW FLOODS DESTROY

Floodwaters are very powerful. They move fast. The water of a flash flood can travel at 20 miles (32 kilometers) per hour or more.

Once they hit land, tsunamis and storm surges cover people and property with frightening speed.

When a river floods, water pours into cities and towns. It gushes into buildings and houses.

Sometimes the worst part of flooding is the cleanup. The floodwater ruins furniture and other possessions. And when the water goes down, a layer of polluted mud covers floors and carpets.

The floodwater dumps sewage and mud into people's houses. Their furniture, appliances, and clothing are ruined.

Rushing waters can whisk away houses and

cars. The water's weight smashes everything in its path. The swift current carries everything along with it. Tree branches, windowpanes, and parts of buildings fly everywhere.

Most flood deaths occur when people are hit by objects swept along by the floodwater. Others die by drowning. Few people can swim against a floodwater's strong currents.

In the floods of 1993, the water treatment plant in Des Moines, Iowa, was put out of service. Trucks brought in clean water for drinking and cooking.

Although water is all around, floodwater is not safe to drink. It is dirty. It contains germs that make people sick. It pours into local water supplies and pollutes them.

A Mississippi River levee
near Burnside, Louisiana (left),
and a seawall at Vancouver,
British Columbia, Canada (right)

FLOOD BARRIERS

Nobody can control the weather that causes floods. So people try to hold water back. They build levees and dikes, flood walls and dams. These structures are called flood barriers.

Levees and dikes are

29

artificial riverbanks made of earth. They are built higher than the river itself so that the river can hold more water. Levees also narrow the river so that water flows faster.

High concrete flood walls are built along riverbanks. They keep water from flowing onto land.

Dams block rivers and streams and stop the flow of water. The water is held in a large lake, or reservoir, created in the

The water backed up by Hoover Dam (left)
in Nevada created Lake Mead (right).

river valley by the dam.
The reservoir water is
released when needed.

The Hoover Dam tames
the Colorado River. The
water held back creates
Lake Mead. Many people
use the lake for recreation. **31**

Left: Water flows down from the reservoir to the power plant through pipes called penstocks. Right: The power plant at Hoover Dam

Water stored in a dam
can be used to make
electricity. First, the water
is released through
pipes called penstocks.
Then the water flows over
32   a wheel called a turbine.

The weight of the water makes the turbine spin. The turbine is connected to a generator that turns. The generator produces electrical power for homes and industry.

But flood barriers do not always work. Flood walls crack and levees overflow. Dams burst, and these breakdowns create flash floods. Some of the worst floods in history have been caused by flood barrier failures.

The terrible destruction of the Johnstown Flood was caused when a dam collapsed. The dam was high in the hills above the town, which was in a narrow valley. The valley walls pushed the water up into a tall wave that struck the town with terrific force.

Over 100 years ago, more than 2,000 people died in Johnstown, Pennsylvania, when a dam burst. The Johnstown Flood was the deadliest flood of its kind in the history of the United States.

DIVERTING WATER

Floods can be prevented by diversion channels. These channels send water in another direction.

Diversion channels are built around parts of a river that often flood. Then the water flows through the channels into another body of water. For example, in New Orleans a diversion channel reroutes water from the Mississippi River into Lake Pontchartrain.

A meteorologist (left) using a computer to track weather conditions. The computer below shows temperatures across the United States at 18,000 feet above the ground.

PREDICTING FLOODS

Meteorologists are scientists who study weather conditions. They predict when floods are likely to happen.

Meteorologists at

weather stations check the flow of rivers. They use instruments called river gauges to predict water height. They use radar to predict rainfall.

Devices called flash flood alarms are attached to river piers. When the river water reaches a certain level, an alarm sounds. This alarm lets people know that a flash flood is about to occur.

At over sixty weather stations in the Pacific

Ocean, scientists study changes in the ocean floor. Certain changes warn that tsunamis may occur.

At the National Hurricane Center in Miami, Florida, meteorologists constantly watch for hurricanes. Satellites and radar help them predict hurricanes.

A meteorologist plots the track of a hurricane at the National Hurricane Center.

FLOOD WATCHES AND WARNINGS

TV stations, radio stations, and newspapers warn people about floods so that they can protect themselves.

Everyone should understand flood warnings and know what they mean. A *flood watch* means that a flood is possible. There is time to prepare for the flood. People should go to a safer area on higher ground.

A bus is caught in a flooded underpass.

A *flood warning* means that a flood will probably occur. People should lock up their houses and head for shelter in a safe area immediately.

During a flood it is important to follow safety rules:

Do not try to walk in

Sometimes floodwaters cover bridges and cut off roads.

floodwater. Do not swim in it.

Never drive over flooded areas. The floodwater may carry the car into deeper areas where it could overturn.

Do not go into a flooded area to see the damage. Do not return to get belongings once you have left.

Throw out any food touched by floodwater. Boil tap water before you use it.

It is important to heed flood warnings and take precautions. Many people have died in floods because they ignored warnings. They did not believe the flood would harm them.

In 1993 heavy rains brought floods to eight

The 1993 flood of the Mississippi River at Valmeyer, Illinois

states. The floods caused
billions of dollars of
damage but few deaths.
Without our excellent
warning systems, many
people would have died.

THE WORLD'S WORST FLOODS

YEAR	PLACE	CAUSE	DEATHS
1824	Russia	River flood	10,000
1876	Bakarganj, India	Cyclone	200,000
1881	India	Cyclone	100,000
1881	Indochina	Typhoon	300,000
1883	Java and Sumatra	Tsunami	36,000
1887	Honan, China	Huang He River overflowed	900,000
1896	Japan	Tsunami	27,000
1931	China	River flood	145,000
1938	North China	Chinese blew up dikes to impede Japanese invasion	1 million
1942	India	Cyclone	40,000
1963	Bangladesh	Cyclone	22,000
1970	Bangladesh	Cyclone	250,000
1987	The Netherlands	Sea storm	50,000

WORST FLOODS IN NORTH AMERICA

DATE	PLACE	CAUSE	DEATHS
1861	California	Sacramento River overflowed	700
1874	Western Massachusetts	Dam failure	144
1889	Johnstown, Pennsylvania	Dam failure	over 2,000
1900	Galveston, Texas	Hurricane	over 6,000
1913	Ohio and Indiana	Ohio River overflowed	732
1926	Mexico	Dam failure	100
1928	Santa Paula, California	Dam failure	450
1929	Canada and Newfoundland	Tidal wave	27
1935	Mexico	Actopan River overflowed	400
1935	Mexico	Flash flood	100
1947	Mexico	Cloudburst	40
1954	Canada	Hurricane	83
1958	Mexico	(not listed)	26
1959	Haiti	Heavy rains	40
1971	Canada	Prolonged rain	31
1972	South Dakota	Dam failure	242
1972	West Virginia	Dam failure	125
1972	Mexico	Cloudburst	30
1973	Mexico City, Mexico	Thunderstorm	37
1976	Colorado	Flash flood of the Big Thompson River	139

WORDS YOU SHOULD KNOW

absorb (ub • ZORB)–to soak up

artificial (ar • tih • FISH • il)–made by people; not natural

barrier (BAIR • ee • yer)–a block; an obstruction that keeps something from moving forward

cloudburst (CLOWD • berst)–a storm in which a large amount of rain falls in a short time

current (KER • int)–a flow of water in a certain direction

dam (DAM)–a structure built across a river to control the flow of water and provide power to make electricity

destructive (dih • STRUK • tiv)–likely to destroy or ruin

dike (DYKE)–a wall built to keep a sea or river from flooding over land

disaster (dih • ZASS • ter)–an event that causes great damage or suffering

disturbance (dih • STER • bince)–a sudden change

diversion (dih • VER • zjun)–used to change direction

divert (dih • VERT)–to turn aside; to change the direction of a movement

earthquake (ERTH • kwaik)–the shaking of the ground caused by movements of rocks deep within the earth

erupt (ih • RUPT)–to burst out; to break out

gauge (GAIJE)–an instrument used to measure the amount of something

germs (JERMZ)–harmful bacteria that cause disease

hurricane (HER • ih • kain)–a strong storm with heavy rain and very high winds

levee (LEH • vee)–a bank of earth built along a river to keep it from overflowing

meteorologist (me • tee • or • AHL • ah • jist)–a scientist who studies weather

minerals (MIN • rilz)–substances in the soil that plants need to grow and be healthy

penstocks (PEN • stox)—pipes in dams that release water for use in making electricity

pollute (puh • LOOT)—to make dirty or poisonous

precautions (prih • KAW • shunz)—measures taken ahead of time to avoid danger

predict (prih • DIKT)—to tell what will happen in the future

radar (RAY • dar)—a device that finds objects by bouncing radio waves off them

reroute (ree • ROWT)—to send in a different direction or to a different place

reservoir (reh • zih • VWAHR)—an artificial lake that holds water for drinking or to make electric power

satellites (SAT • ill • ites)—a body, such as a moon, that revolves around a planet

saturated (SAT • cher • ay • tid)—completely soaked; holding as much water as it can

sewage (SOO • widj)—wastewater from houses and factories

storm surge (STORM SERJ)—a huge wave of water that comes onto land during a hurricane

torrential (tor • REN • shill)—overwhelming; like a torrent

tsunami (soo • NAH • mee)—a very high wave that comes onshore after an undersea earthquake or volcanic eruption

turbine (TER • byne)—an engine that is made to turn by the pressure of water or gas

valuable (VAL • yoo • ah • bil)—having great value; precious

volcano (vawl • KAY • no)—an opening in the Earth's crust through which material from inside the Earth erupts

INDEX

About the Author

Arlene Erlbach has written more than a dozen books for young people in many genres including fiction and nonfiction.

She has a master's degree in special education. In addition to being an author of children's books, she is a learning disabilities teacher at Gray School in Chicago, Illinois. Arlene loves to encourage children to write and is in charge of her school's Young Authors program.

For LINDA

A "POS" person -

The Three Robots

by

Art Fettig

Illustrated by Joe Carpenter

Dedicated to all those who want
to continue growing up, up, up.
Special thanks to Suzy Sutton
for helping me grow.

Published by Growth Unlimited
31 East Ave. South
Battle Creek, Michigan 49017

Manufactured in the United States of America
Designed by Sandy Mol

Library of Congress Catalog Card Number 80-84356
Fettig, Art
The Three Robots

ISBN
1 2 3 4 5 6 7 8 9 0

Once upon a time, not far away, in the land of Tomorrow lived three robots.

The one named Pos was a happy robot. A robot with a bright shining smile. A successful robot, always filled with energy.

3

She thought happy, positive thoughts, and things generally turned out right for Pos. If you had to describe Pos with one symbol it would be a plus sign. "+"

Semi-pos was not happy, not sad. He didn't smile and he didn't frown. He wore a blank expression. He was a robot who was not sure of his feelings. Semi-pos was sometimes described as "A Pos with a pause." If you talked with him you would often hear him say, "Tomorrow," "Not now," "Later!" "Mañana," and "Someday." His favorite word was "Gonna," and his favorite expression was "When I get around to it."

Semi-pos was never quite sure what he should do about anything, and so, generally, he just put things off.

A good way to describe Semi-pos would be with a question mark. "?"

Neg was a sad robot. He never won. Never even dreamed he might win. He believed he was programmed for failure and he never got out of step.

Neg always wore a sad look on his face. He was a tired robot, even when he had lots of rest. The best symbol for Neg would be a minus sign. "−"

All three robots lived nearby, and from behind they looked like most other robots. You might not know which was which.

But if they turned around you'd know. They were different up front.

9

Pos was an earlier model, rather plain looking. Still
she contained all of the necessary components to function
in a modern manner.

Semi-pos was not the latest model on the market, but his inner workings were more condensed, lighter, and he could be programmed for a wider variety of activities than Pos. His head and shoulders had been streamlined with more chrome and fancy trim.

Neg was the newest robot on the market, light, flexible, his solar input screens were larger and his energy storage units had twice the capacity to store the sun's power than Pos's or Semi-pos's could store. Outside Neg wore a new dome light and fancy stripes which his designer believed added a new sleek look.

But, it was on their faces that you could see the real difference.

Pos wore a smile. Her teeth were brushed and
flossed. She cared about the way she looked to others.

Semi-pos wore a blank expression. No smile. And since no one saw his teeth, he brushed them only now and then and he never flossed.

And Neg wore a frown. He never ever smiled and so he felt there was no need to maintain his teeth. Who cared? Who would see them anyway?

One day the three robots were together in the park, and Pos was saying happy things like, "It really is a wonderful day. I'm so lucky to be alive."

And Semi-pos was not sure about the weather or anything else. "Maybe it will rain," he said. "Maybe."

Neg just knew that something bad would probably happen to him and so he continued to be sad. Soon something would happen to make him unhappy. He just knew it. And he was seldom wrong.

Pos sat down on the bench next to Semi-pos, and after a long moment, Semi-pos turned to Pos and asked, "Pos, why are you always so happy?"

And Pos replied, "Because it feels so good to be happy."

Semi-pos just sat there for a while looking confused
and then Pos said to Semi-pos, "Why don't you try it?
It's fun being happy."

And Semi-pos scratched his elbow nervously and
finally he replied, "I don't know. Maybe I will try feeling
happy sometime. Perhaps I'll try it tomorrow. Or maybe
the day after tomorrow. Someday. But not right now."

"Now!" Pos said. "Won't you please try it now?" Pos put her hand on her friend's shoulder to encourage him. "Say something happy. Tell me how good you feel and how much you like it here in the park."

"Not now," Semi-pos said. "I'm gonna do it, just as soon as I get around to it, but not right now."

Just then Neg walked over to the park bench and
joined the other robots.

"How about you, Neg?" Pos asked. "How would you
like to try being happy today?"

Neg shook his head. "Not me. There is nothing in this world for me to be happy about. Not today. Not ever. I was just put here to be sad, and that's the way it is."

Neg frowned and just ignored Pos as she smiled her warmest, brightest smile. And Neg walked away.

Semi-pos turned to Pos and tried to smile, but his lips did not know how. "Besides," he thought, "my teeth are dirty today and Pos would see them if I smiled."

"Maybe tomorrow, Pos," he said, "I might try being happy tomorrow. We'll see."

Pos went home and sat alone and thought about her two friends. "Why were they so different? Why was Semi-pos so unsure, so uncertain about himself and his actions? And why was Neg so sad, so unwilling to try for happiness? Why wouldn't Semi-pos smile?"

"Why?" she pondered. "Why couldn't her friends see that it was so much easier to be happy than to be sad, that smiling and winning were easy and fun once you set your mind to it." Pos sighed and thought to herself, "Being happy is nice, but it would be a lot more fun if I could share that feeling of happiness with my friends." She'd try again tomorrow.

It was now morning and Pos carefully checked out all her systems. They were functioning beautifully.

Once when she had not been in the sun all day, she had forgotten to attach her recharging system during the dark period, and the next day she had felt worn down and somewhat lifeless. Since then she always made sure that each day she got plenty of sunshine on her solar input units. She didn't want to feel run down again, ever. And she never did.

It was easy to stay happy and full of life once you knew the secret. Daily sunshine provided the energy for a robot's healthy life.

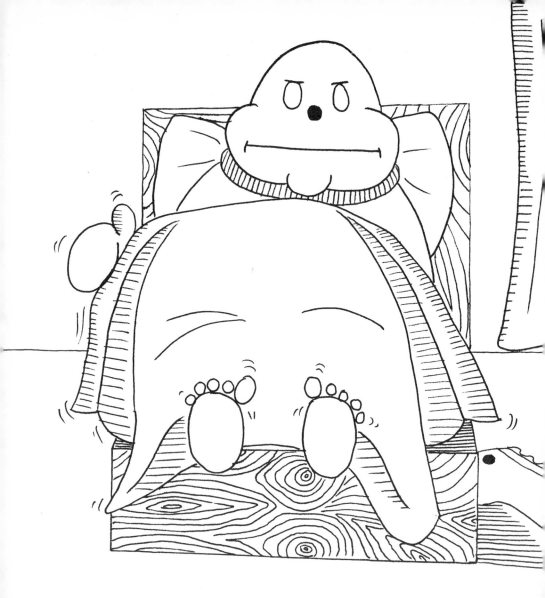

Semi-pos wasn't sure how to feel this morning. It
might be a good day to be happy, but he wasn't certain.
Perhaps tomorrow would be better. How did he feel?
Everything seemed to be functioning okay, and, yet,
there was nothing special about that fact. After all,
weren't robots built to function properly?

Neg felt logy. He didn't welcome this new day at all. Not this day or any day. What was the meaning of this thing called life? He knew it would be a bad day. Something was certain to go wrong again. Didn't it always? Losing was his nature.

Things might have gone on that way, with Neg living a sad, unhappy existence, Semi-pos putting off until tomorrow all the things he'd like to do... someday, and Pos enjoying every moment of every day. Life might have gone on that way, but something very important happened that particular morning. Something that would change the lives of the robots forever.

Pos took a good look at Neg. Then Pos took another look at Neg. She squinted her eyes and reached out and felt the back of Neg's head.

"What's that clasp on the back of your head for, Neg?" she asked.

"What clasp?" Neg replied. "I don't know anything about a clasp on the back of my head. I've never even seen the back of my head. How could I do that? My eyes are on the front of my head, just like yours, Pos."

The robots all laughed, only now Neg and Semi-pos
began to examine the back of each other's head.

"You've got a clasp alright," Semi-pos said to Neg.

"And you've got one too, Pos. What's it for?"

"Who knows!" Pos replied.

"Come here, Neg, Let me turn the clasp and see what happens."

"Won't it hurt?" Neg asked.

"I'll do it slowly," Pos suggested, "if it hurts, just tell me and I will stop."

Pos carefully turned the clasp and immediately a panel flipped down revealing a screen on the back of Neg's head. The screen looked very much like a small television set!

37

On the screen were words like those found on a computer printout tube. Neg's screen was filled with negative words. "Don't." " Shouldn't." "Can't." "Never." "Lose." "Give up." "Unhappy." "Frown."

Neg could not see his own printout screen and so he
reached back to hide his thoughts. "Don't look at mine,"
Neg said. "Let me see yours, Semi-pos."
Semi-pos looked confused. "Not now," he said.

"What about yours, Pos?" Neg asked. "I'll show you mine if you show me yours."

Pos nodded. "Why not?" She turned her head so that Neg could unfasten the clasp on her panel. She smiled at Neg and asked, "What does mine say?"

Neg read the panel slowly. "It says, 'Can.' 'Will.' 'Happy.' 'Win.' 'Easy does it.' 'Yes.' and 'Smile.' "

41

Together the two robots turned to Semi-pos who had been peeking at Pos's panel as Neg read the words on her screen.

"How about it, Semi-pos?" Pos asked. "Do we get to see yours?"

"I'm not sure," Semi-pos replied, "perhaps we should wait."

Pos did not ask further. She simply reached around to the back of Semi-pos's head and unfastened the clasp. Both robots then read the words on Semi-pos's printout tube. "Gonna," it read. "Someday." "Not now." "Put it off." "When I get around to it."

"What does it say?" Semi-pos asked. And so Pos and Neg slowly read Semi-pos his mind.

For a long time the robots just sat there looking at each other's screens, trying to understand what they had discovered.

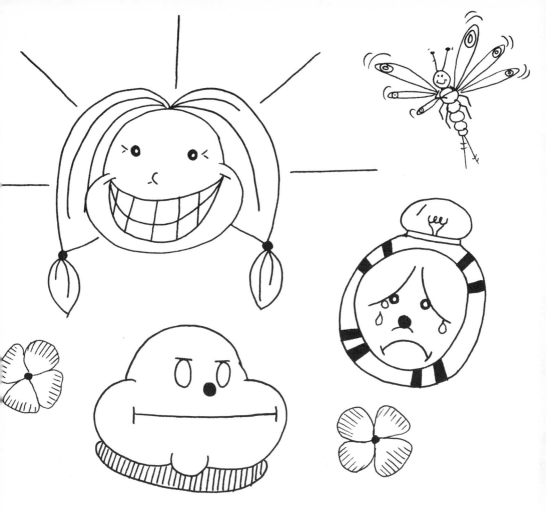

Suddenly the answer came to Pos and she shared it with her friends.

"We are programmed," she explained. "Our minds are programmed like computers. You read my mind and it is filled with only positive words. Neg, your words are all negative. And Semi-pos, yours are all delay-action thoughts. If our minds are programmed with thoughts, then perhaps we can feed good ideas into our minds. Then we might all be happy together."

Neg just shook his head. "I'll never be happy," he said. "Nothing will ever be right for me," he sighed.

"It is a great idea," Semi-pos said. "And someday we'll try it. Someday, when I get around to it, we'll do it."

Pos spent the rest of the day thinking about her friends. She would find some way to put happiness into their lives. If only she could change the words on their screens.

That was it! Change the words! And suddenly Pos
had an idea.

All that next morning she worked on her secret plan. She took a broomstick and cut off a thin circle of wood. With a wood-burning tool she burned a short message on the wooden chip, and after the word was burned deeply into the disc, she took sandpaper and polished the object very carefully. She worked at it until the chip was perfectly round and smooth. Now she had her present, but she would have to find the right moment to give it to Semi-pos.

And so she waited, watched and listened. Unknowingly Semi-pos was very cooperative.

It was not long before the perfect situation developed. It was early afternoon and Pos had the present in her robot hand, waiting for the right moment. The robots were talking about taking a new look at each other's screens when Pos smiled at Semi-pos and asked, "How about it, Semi-pos? Do you want to try smiling today?"

And as usual, Semi-pos answered, "Not now. Someday. Someday I'll try smiling. Someday when I get around to it."

53

This was the moment Pos had been waiting for.
"Well then," she said, "here's a present for you Semi-pos.
I made you a round TUIT."

And with that Pos handed Semi-pos the round
wooden chip on which she had burned the word "TUIT."
"It is a round TUIT, Semi-pos. You are always saying
you will do it when you get around to it. So now you
have a round TUIT and there's no longer any reason for
you not to do it!"

55

Semi-pos took the round TUIT in his robot hand. He just stood there thinking for a moment. He shrugged his shoulders and suddenly a new expression began to form on his face. His lips quivered a bit, and then he did it. Semi-pos smiled.

It was a weak smile at first, but once his face got the message his smile grew broader and broader and soon he wore what must have been the broadest, friendliest, happiest smile a robot had ever smiled.

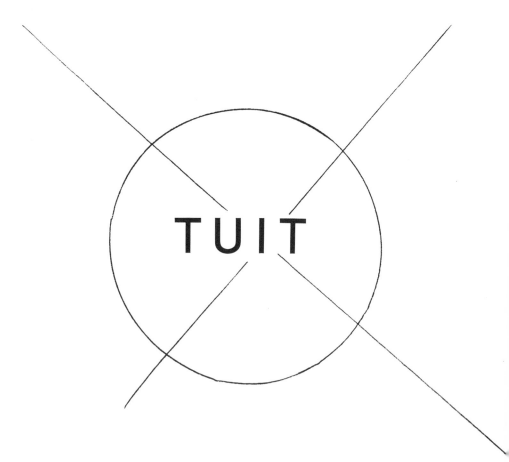

TUIT

57

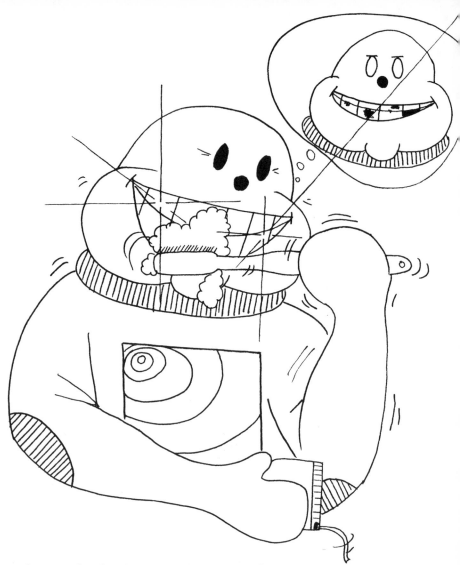

The night before and again that morning, Semi-pos
had worked hard on brushing his teeth and flossing. He
remembered how he was ashamed of his dirty teeth
earlier. And now he let his happy feeling take over and
fill his whole face with a bright shining, wonderful smile
And that smile went out to the world, but at the same
time the feeling behind that smile invaded Semi-pos's
whole being.

"I feel happy, Pos," he said. "For the first time in my life I truly feel happy and I don't think I will ever want to feel sad again."

The two robots, Pos and Semi-pos, stood there for a long while, just smiling back and forth, silently sharing with each other that good feeling that was now inside them. And then, as both their hearts were near overflowing with joy, they suddenly thought of Neg.

Neg was particularly unhappy. At first when he saw Semi-pos smiling that bright and wonderful smile, he did not recognize him. Neg thought that perhaps a new robot had joined their group. But once he discovered that it was Semi-pos smiling, a whole new kind of sadness overcame him.

"Why must I be the loser? The unhappy one? Why
must my screen be filled with so many negative thoughts
and words and ideas? I wonder," he thought, "I wonder
what Semi-pos's screen looks like right now."

And so he walked right up to Semi-pos and asked,
"Semi-pos, would you mind if I looked at your screen
right now? I just wonder if it has changed because you
are smiling."

Semi-pos thought it was a splendid idea, since he too
wondered about his screen. Neg turned the clasp, the
panel covering Semi-pos's screen opened and Neg was
amazed at what he saw. "Look Pos!" he cried, "It has all
changed."

There in the center of the screen was a giant
round TUIT and faintly behind the big word were
the words, "Gonna" and "Someday."

They both read the words on the screen to Semi-pos.
"What does it mean, Pos?" he asked.

"It means that we must keeping working." Pos
replied. "We must make your positive thoughts so stron
that they will overwhelm those delay-action ideas that
are still there on your screen."

"But how?" Semi-pos asked.

"Keep your round TUIT and keep saying, 'I'm
happy, I'm healthy, I'm successful.' We must work on it
every day. It is so easy to forget."

"Do you do that, Pos?" Semi-pos asked.

"Certainly, I do. My mind needs reminding. Things
don't always go right. And you run into those who do
not have happy thoughts. But if you continue to put
positive thoughts into your mind every day, you can
always find happiness."

"What about it, Pos?" Semi-pos asked. "Do you
believe we can ever make Neg happy?"

"Only if he truly wants to be happy," Pos answered.
"It must be his own idea."

Time passed and Pos and Semi-pos worked daily on their positive thoughts and they both worked on brushing their teeth and flossing so that their smiles would continue to be bright and wonderful.

These were lonely days for Neg. Before, he had his
friend Semi-pos to frown at and be unhappy with. But
now, Semi-pos wore a bright smile on his face every day.
Before, Pos was the odd one, but now only Neg wore a
frown. At first he just ignored it. But soon he began to
resent his unhappiness.

Both Pos and Semi-pos told him they believed he
could find happiness, with their help, if he desired it. But
everything in Neg's head told him that smiling and
happiness was for other robots, not for him.

And then one morning he was alone with Pos and he asked Pos to read once more what was there on his screen.

Pos did not like this job, but she truly wanted to help her friend. She knew that sometimes you had to do unpleasant things to help someone you love. She read the words to Neg very slowly. "Don't." "Shouldn't." "Can't." "Never." "Won't." "Isn't." "Lose." "Give up." "Frown."

Neg frowned. "Those are bad words, aren't they, Pos?"

Pos smiled warmly and tried to be gentle.

"Let's say that they aren't the words I would want on my screen." she said.

"But what can we do about them?" Neg asked.

"What do you want to do about them, Neg?"

68

A sad wistful look came over Neg's face, and now the tears poured down his cheeks. "I'd like to change," he sobbed. "I want to laugh and smile and be happy just like you and Semi-pos."

"Good," Pos said. "I believe that we are all engineered to be happy. Let's find a way to change those words."

They started the next morning. The three robots joined hands and sang this song together.

"I'm healthy, I'm happy,
I am somebody.
Not a sad nobody
I am somebody.
And I wear a smile
Just to let the whole world know
That this somebody's happy inside."

And as they sang both Pos and Semi-pos smiled and their hearts were filled with joy, but Neg continued to frown and feel miserable.

"I'm not healthy," he sobbed. "My screen is filled with sick words. I'm unhappy and I'm still a nobody."

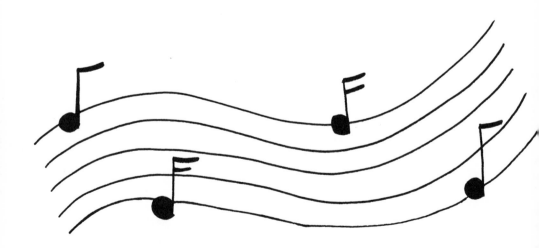

"It takes time," Pos explained. "You won't change overnight. Be patient."

"Why do you and Semi-pos have such happy bright smiles?" Neg asked.

Pos laughed. "Because we work on them. We brush our teeth three times a day and we floss between our teeth every day to keep our teeth really clean." And then Pos gave Neg a lesson on brushing and flossing. Pos smiled at her friend. "Neg," she said, "you just might want to get your teeth ready for smiling. You never know when happiness will come into your life."

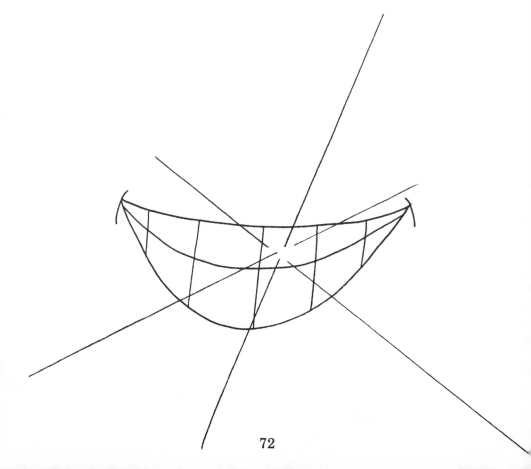

The days and the nights passed and Pos and Semi-pos tried every means of encouragement and persuasion they could find, but nothing seemed to work with Neg. They consulted the Robot Operations Manual, but there was nothing written on smiling or being happy. Happiness was something new that Pos had discovered for herself.

Then one day Neg gave up all hope. "I'll never be happy or smile like the other robots," he thought. "It would be best if I went away. That way I won't be reminded of how unhappy I really am. Besides, I think I'm making Pos and Semi-pos unhappy because they aren't able to find a way to help me change."

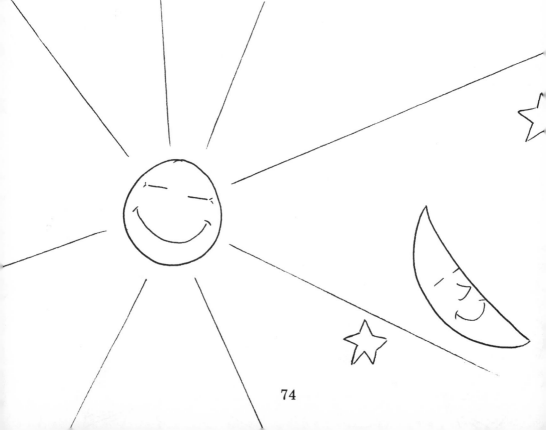

And so early the next morning Neg quietly and
quickly packed his bag, and before the other robots saw
him, he rushed out of their lives.

He walked alone for hours, and the farther away
from his friends he went, the sadder he became. He never
knew that a robot could ever be so sad and lonely, and
finally he just sat down by the roadside and cried.

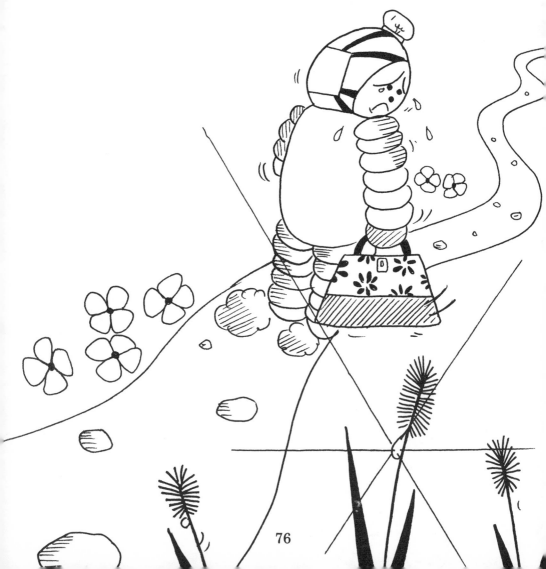

Neg had no idea of how long he had been sitting there. Perhaps an hour or maybe a day. Time spent in suffering alone passes very slowly. Finally, Neg thought about his screen. He knew it must now be filled with words even more negative than before, if that be possible.

"But if it is possible for me to make myself even more miserable and unhappy than I was before," he thought, "then just maybe Pos is right. Maybe I can make myself happy if I try hard enough."

Neg sat by the roadside concentrating on the one phrase, "I'm happy." He said it aloud, "I'm happy." Now he shouted it. "I'M HAPPY!" He realized that if he was to become happy, he must try to act as if he truly was happy, even if he was not. The tears were rolling down his cheeks freely now. He said it again and again. "I'm happy. I'm happy. I'm happy. I'm happy."

And suddenly he did not feel quite so miserable.

Neg found a small stream alongside the road and he washed the tears off his face and then he took the time to brush his teeth and floss once more. He'd been working on keeping his teeth clean ever since Pos showed him how. He wanted to be prepared to smile a bright wonderful smile if someday he ever did find happiness.

Now he tried it again. "I'M HAPPY!" he cried out. "Yes, I am happy." He sighed. "I don't have any reason to be happy yet, but that doesn't matter. The reason for my happiness will come later. I must first get the message to my screen."

Neg worked on that one idea for the rest of the day and finally his energy level began to run low because sadness and negative thinking uses up a robot's energy quickly.

Since he was far away from his home, he had no place to recharge his energy cells. He would have to wait for the sun's bright rays to renew him. The dark period was coming quickly and so Neg just laid down by the side of the road to rest.

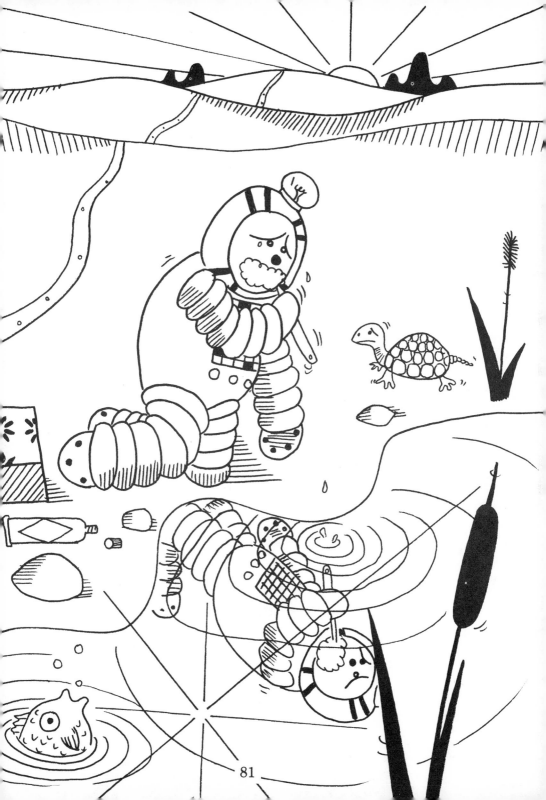

Over and over he repeated that one message to his mind. "I'm happy. I'm happy. I'm happy."

Yet tears of unhappiness covered his face and he knew that the words were not yet written on his screen. He went to sleep hoping that those words would change.

The hot sunshine woke Neg, but his energy level was still so low he could hardly move. He opened his eyes and his first thought was on that message he wanted so badly to be written on his screen. "I'm happy." He thought and then he tried to shout it out, but he was just too weak to shout.

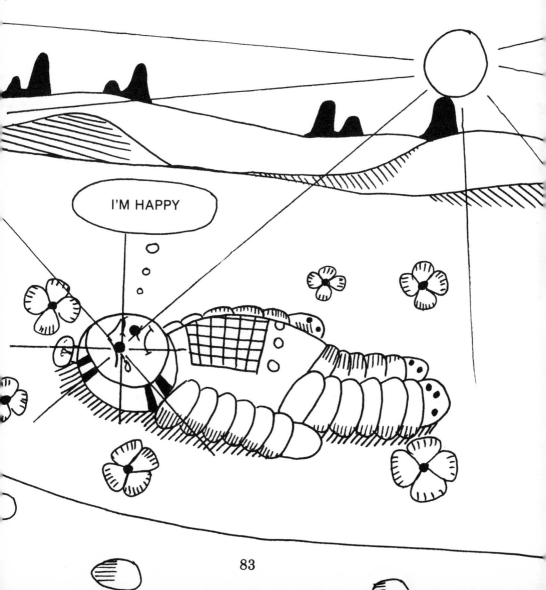

Neg thought he heard the voices of his friends
coming from far down the road. The voices were faint at
first, but as they drew nearer they grew stronger and
stronger. He heard the cry, "Neg... where are you, Neg?"
And with all his remaining energy Neg cried out, "I'm
here, Pos. I'm here."

Both Pos and Semi-pos ran to greet their friend.

"Neg," Semi-pos cried, "you didn't have to leave us.
We've searched for you since we found you'd gone."

Neg drew up his energy for a moment and then he said it aloud for them to hear. "I'm happy!" He said it softly and the thought of it renewed his strength. Now he shouted it out for the world to hear. "I'M HAPPY!"

Pos and Semi-pos hugged their friend. "We are so glad we found you, Neg." Pos said.

And as Neg raised his head and climbed to his feet he felt it happening.

For the first time in his existence, Neg smiled. He looked very strange with such a broad, shining, wonderful smile on his face, because tears were now pouring down his cheeks. Tears of joy. And he was not alone for now the other robots were crying too.

And the three robots joined hands and shouted out
together, "We are healthy, we are happy, we are
successful!"

They sat by the roadside together, letting the warm
sunshine renew their energy cells and finally Neg turned
to Pos and asked, "Pos, will you look at my screen and
tell me what it says?"

And Pos turned the clasp, the panel dropped open, and the three robots shared their happiness as Pos read the screen.

"I'm happy!" the screen read. And there were still some negatives words on the screen, but the brightest biggest word of all was "HAPPY!"

And in time both Semi-pos and Neg would have screens bright with positive and happy words, for now they knew that they could put whatever words they wished on their screens.

And from that day on, every morning, the robots would meet in the park and sing their song,

> "We're healthy, we're happy,
> We are somebody,
> Not a sad nobody,
> We are somebody,
> And we wear a smile...."

89

The two robots, Pos and Semi-pos, looked at Neg and Neg smiled a bright happy smile at them both, and then it happened, the dome light on Neg's head began flashing on and off as if to celebrate the happiness inside him. They all laughed and then they continued singing,

> "And we wear a smile
> Just to let the whole world know,
> That this somebody's happy inside."

And the robot who was the very happiest inside and outside and wore the broadest, happiest smile of all was Pos, because, now she had two friends with whom to share her happiness.

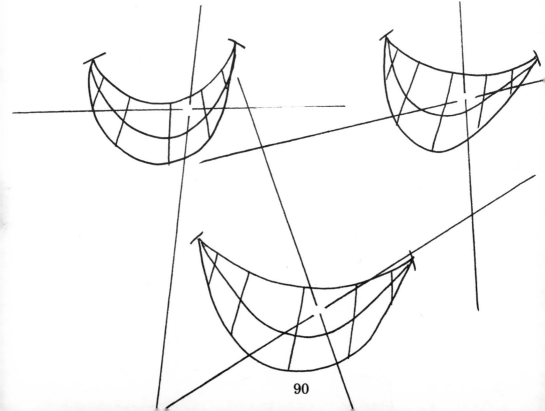

Dear Reader:

You can be happy every day too. And you can wear the kind of smile that lets the whole world know that yo are really happy inside.

To have a bright happy and wonderful smile, all you have to do is form the habit of good daily tooth care. It is easy when you brush three times each day and get the good habit of flossing daily.

And what better time to feed those happy thoughts into your own mind. You know, your mind works the very same way as the minds of the three robots. If you feed your mind happy, successful thoughts every day, then you will be happy and successful.

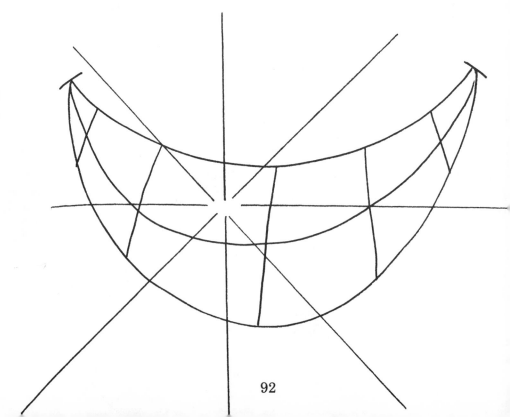

As you brush your teeth each morning why not sing the robot song.

"We are healthy, we're happy,
We're somebody... Not a sad nobody,
No, we're somebody...
And we wear a smile
(The brightest happiest smile ever,)
Just to let the whole world know,
That this somebody's happy inside."

10 Positive Attitude Discussion Questions

Q. Why do you think that Pos was such a happy robot?

Q. What happens when you act the way Semi-pos acted? Do you put things off until tomorrow that you might better do today?

Q. Why didn't Semi-pos want Pos to see him smiling?

Q. What might you do to make sure that you always have a bright shining smile?

Q. Why did the robots meet every day to sing their song?

Q. What finally made Neg happy?

Q. Why do you think that Pos was the happiest robot of all?

Q. If you had to rate yourself today do you think you are more like Pos, Semi-pos or Neg? Why?

Q. What do you think your screen looks like? Would you like to change some of the words?

Q. If you want to be happy, how do you think you might start?

About the author

Art Fettig is a professional communicator. He is a
prolific writer whose work has been published in hundreds
of magazines. His books include "It Only Hurts When I
Frown" Liguori Press, 1973; "Selling Lucky, A Guide to
Greater Success & Happiness," Frederick Fell Publisher,
1978; "Anatomy of a Speech," Ovations Unlimited, 1978;
"How to Hold an Audience in the Hollow of your Hand,"
Frederick Fell Publisher, 1979.

He is a recording artist with cassette tape albums
available on the following subjects: Speaking, Selling
your Writing, Safety, Lucky Ideas and Real Estate Sales.

His filmstrip productions on railroad crossing safety
are seen by millions of students yearly and are used
extensively in school bus driver training.

He is a regular contributor to Positive Living
Magazine and to the Self Development Journal.

Art Fettig is a nationally known speaker and he
addresses over 100 audiences each year in the fields of
sales, motivation, creativity, safety and humor.

This is Mr. Fettig's first venture in the children's
literature field. "Most of what we do in the field of
positive thinking is corrective," Fettig explains. "We
take people's lives that are not what they want them to
be and try to show them how to change. I believe that

we can help our children have a positive self image from the start and I hope that my series of children's books will help make that a reality."

Fettig lives with Ruth, his wife of over 25 years, at : East Avenue South, Battle Creek, Michigan, 49017 and can be reached at (616) 966-5329 or (616) 964-4821.